THE GRANDEST RIDE

Tom Brownold

Text by **Brad Dimock**

RIO NUEVO
PUBLISHERS
TUCSON, ARIZONA

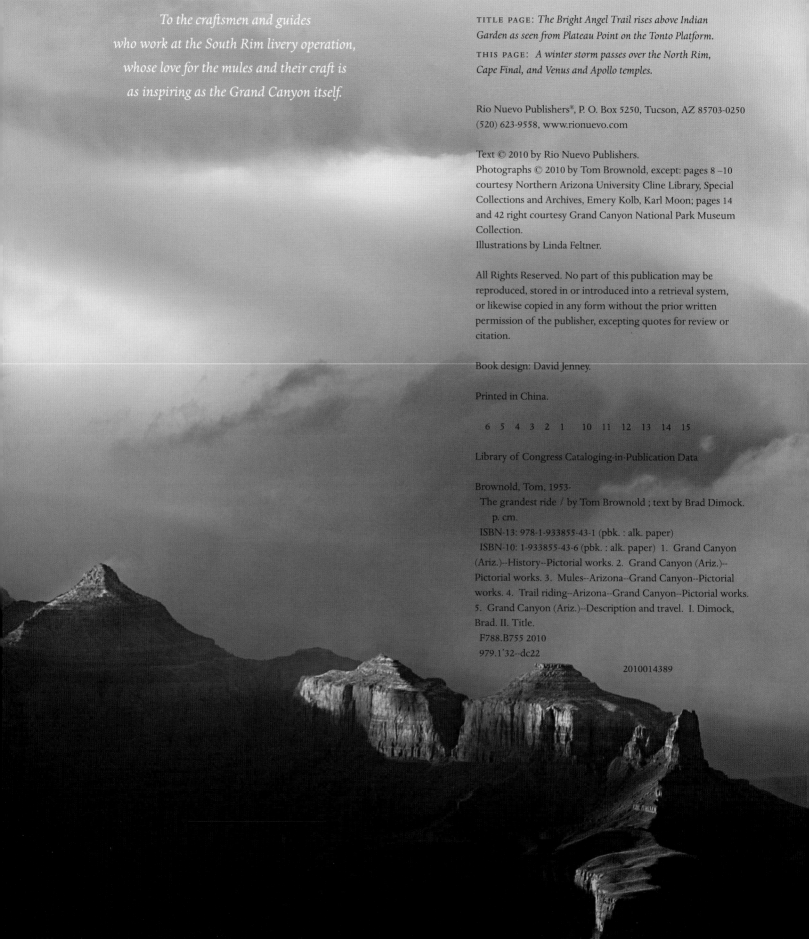

*To the craftsmen and guides
who work at the South Rim livery operation,
whose love for the mules and their craft is
as inspiring as the Grand Canyon itself.*

TITLE PAGE: *The Bright Angel Trail rises above Indian Garden as seen from Plateau Point on the Tonto Platform.*
THIS PAGE: *A winter storm passes over the North Rim, Cape Final, and Venus and Apollo temples.*

Rio Nuevo Publishers®, P. O. Box 5250, Tucson, AZ 85703-0250
(520) 623-9558, www.rionuevo.com

Text © 2010 by Rio Nuevo Publishers.
Photographs © 2010 by Tom Brownold, except: pages 8 –10 courtesy Northern Arizona University Cline Library, Special Collections and Archives, Emery Kolb, Karl Moon; pages 14 and 42 right courtesy Grand Canyon National Park Museum Collection.
Illustrations by Linda Feltner.

Book design: David Jenney.

Printed in China.

6   5   4   3   2   1   10   11   12   13   14   15

Library of Congress Cataloging-in-Publication Data

Brownold, Tom, 1953-
   The grandest ride / by Tom Brownold ; text by Brad Dimock.
      p. cm.
   ISBN-13: 978-1-933855-43-1 (pbk. : alk. paper)
   ISBN-10: 1-933855-43-6 (pbk. : alk. paper) 1. Grand Canyon (Ariz.)--History--Pictorial works. 2. Grand Canyon (Ariz.)--Pictorial works. 3. Mules--Arizona--Grand Canyon--Pictorial works. 4. Trail riding--Arizona--Grand Canyon--Pictorial works. 5. Grand Canyon (Ariz.)--Description and travel. I. Dimock, Brad. II. Title.
   F788.B755 2010
   979.1`32--dc22
                                   2010014389

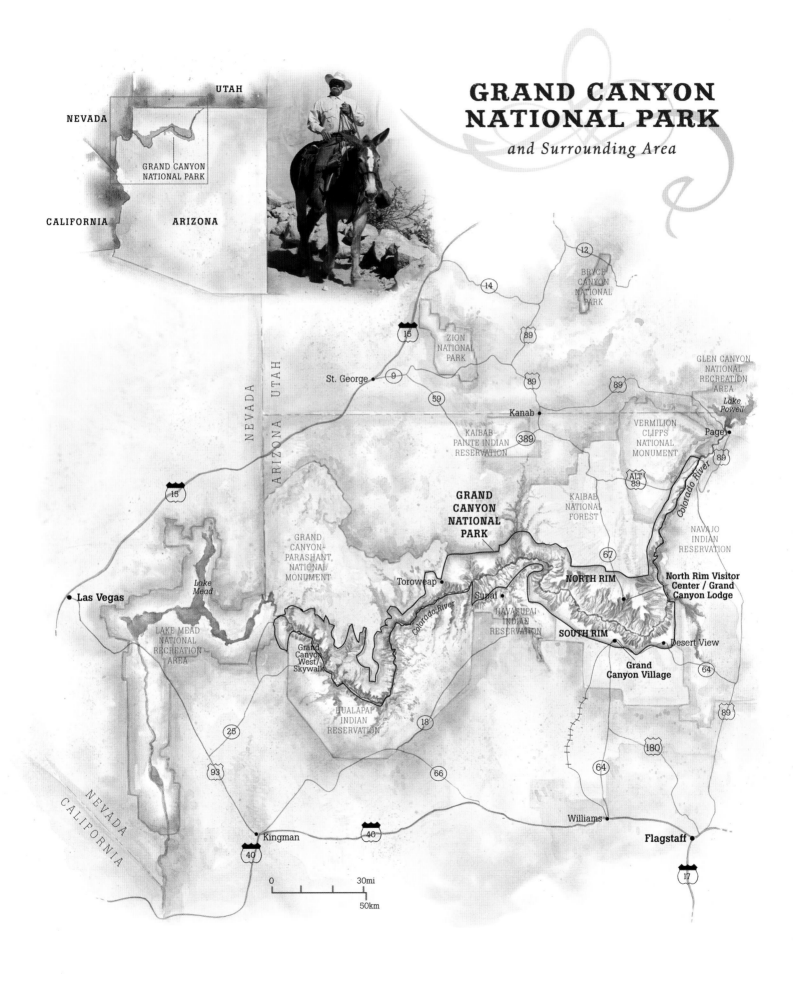

GRAND CANYON NATIONAL PARK

and Surrounding Area

UTAH

NEVADA

GRAND CANYON
NATIONAL PARK

CALIFORNIA   ARIZONA

12

14

BRYCE
CANYON
NATIONAL
PARK

15

ZION
NATIONAL
PARK

89

GLEN CANYON
NATIONAL
RECREATION
AREA

St. George   9

89

Lake
Powell

59

Kanab

89

Page

89

389

KAIBAB-
PAIUTE INDIAN
RESERVATION

VERMILION
CLIFFS
NATIONAL
MONUMENT

ALT
89

15

**GRAND
CANYON
NATIONAL
PARK**

KAIBAB
NATIONAL
FOREST

Colorado River

NAVAJO
INDIAN
RESERVATION

GRAND
CANYON-
PARASHANT
NATIONAL
MONUMENT

67

Lake
Mead

Toroweap

Supai

NORTH RIM

**North Rim Visitor
Center / Grand
Canyon Lodge**

Las Vegas

Colorado River

HAVASUPAI
INDIAN
RESERVATION

SOUTH RIM

Desert View

LAKE MEAD
NATIONAL
RECREATION
AREA

Grand
Canyon
West/
Skywalk

**Grand
Canyon Village**

64

HUALAPAI
INDIAN
RESERVATION

18

25

89

93

66

180

64

Williams

NEVADA

CALIFORNIA

Kingman

40

Flagstaff

40

17

0   30mi

50km

OVER THE PRECIPICE

I NORMALLY VIEW THE WORLD from about six feet off the ground. This morning my eyes are nine feet above the trail and wobbling as Wyatt, my mule, plods nonchalantly down the steep, icy track. He shows no apparent concern about slipping over the hundred-foot lip inches to the left of his hooves. Grand Canyon, in all its sheer majesty, wheels by in front of me as Wyatt makes the corner, swinging his head out over the canyon as he rounds the point. We've just started down the Bright Angel Trail, which begins at a point on the South Rim nearly a vertical mile above the river. It is some six miles across to the North Rim, the chasm between filled with multi-hued buttes and spires fading into the lavender haze of distance. This stark beauty is lost on me, framed between two long, flopping mule ears as Wyatt switchbacks down the precipice.

I know this ride has been operated for over a century without losing a dude, I know mules are among the most sure-footed of all beasts, and I know I should just relax in my saddle and enjoy the view. But I am gripped, clutching my saddle horn like the greenest of all dudes. Gripped but still laughing.

First light at the South Rim on a frigid morning.

There is something inescapably comical about mules. Even the word mule (from the Latin *mulus*, meaning—what else?—"mule") has an amusing ring. *Myooool.* And the way those long, ludicrous ears flop as they walk. Amusing, yet inscrutable. At the corral this morning before we saddled up, the mules stared at us, silently waiting. Contemplating atrocities? Perhaps. "A mule will labor ten years willingly and patiently for you," wrote William Faulkner, "for the privilege of kicking you once."

ABOVE: *This mule may be planning mischief, but for now it poses for the camera with a wrangler.*
LEFT: *The combination of a donkey and a horse creates a beautiful and hardy animal.*

The sterile offspring of a male donkey and a female horse, the mule is often larger, stronger, healthier, more intelligent, and more efficient than either of its parents—a classic example of what biologists call "hybrid vigor." But it isn't that they're more agile than a horse, claims Larry Spain, who has worked every aspect of Grand Canyon's mule operation off and on for nearly four decades. "They're just more cautious. They have a very strong self-preservation instinct, more so than a horse. You can't make 'em do something to endanger themselves—they'll just stop and that'll be the end of it. Where a horse'll kill himself for ya, a mule, he's just gonna give you what he wants and that's it. Their eyes bulge way out like a burro's, so they can see all four

ABOVE: *A guide and his string leave the South Rim barn to meet the dudes of the day.*
RIGHT: *A farrier gives a mule a new studded shoe.*

feet at once when the footing is bad. They got courser bones in their legs than a horse, and they take that old steep trail better. They don't lose their mind like a horse will when somethin' happens. I mean they don't go plumb crazy—a horse'll run off a cliff, where a mule just locks up. They do really well here." When the trail is icy, as it is this frigid morning

near winter solstice, the mules have large gobs of tungsten carbide welded to their shoes—studded snow tires. So really, there is nothing to worry about. I'm safer up here than I would be walking. Right. Wyatt rounds the next corner and walks the very edge for a few steps, just for effect. I'm still clenched.

Everything about the mule ride is an anachronism—a lost piece of the Old West. The mule barn is over a hundred years old, older than the national park, with several of the main support posts chewed clear through by relentless, mischievous mules.

There is something timeless about the whole operation. It's not just a matter of corralling a bunch of ornery mules at the rim and sending them off the edge each day. Pancho, the livery manager, has a staff of seven to ten wranglers and packers, and about 150–170 mules, male and female, of all sizes and colors, each of which he knows by name and disposition, and each imported by time machine from the 19th century. And there's Joe Marshall, a full-time saddle maker, stationed in his archaic workshop full of leather and arcane toolery. Joe is absolutely in love with his work: building saddles, repairing saddles, and making saddles fit the large variety of mule backs in the herd. "Leather," he assures me, "is the most amazing substance on earth. It can do anything." On the other side of the wall from Joe is the longest continuously operating blacksmith shop in the United States, where two farriers shoe, on the average, five mules a day. After each mule is shod, it gets a haircut. Its shaggy mane is trimmed short and its tail gets trimmed into a series of bell-shapes. When a mule's tail begins looking a bit shaggy, it's time to check its shoes.

ABOVE: *The livery manager inspects the dude mules' tack prior to mounting up the riders for the day.* LEFT: *Farriers shoe mules in the livery stables.*

OVERLEAF: *The Abyss overlook on the South Rim offers a staggering, almost vertical view down into the canyon.*

LAYERS OF HISTORY

Beginning in the 1880s, tourists often went down the trail to the river, but rarely on foot. In those days, hiking wasn't something one did for fun. It was déclassé. Besides, before there were cars, nearly everyone was accustomed to sitting in a saddle. John Hance, the first Anglo to settle at Grand Canyon, gave up his early attempts to make a living here by mining in favor of digging for gold in the pockets of tourists. He advertised on the railway seventy miles to the south and brought clients to the South Rim via a rugged buggy ride. They stayed at his primitive hotel and often went—by mule—down to the river for a night. Thirty miles west, William Wallace Bass followed suit, one-upping Hance with a rim-to-rim connection. Both men augmented their guiding with tales of questionable veracity. "There are three great liars in Grand Canyon," Hance often said. "I am one of them. Bill Bass is the other two."

French-Canadian Louis Boucher followed their lead and opened a trail system from Hermits Rest to the river, leading folks into the canyon on the back of his great white mule, Silver Bell. Ralph Cameron, later a senator, began developing mining prospects along the Bright Angel fault. When he and his partners realized, like those before them, that the real money was in tourists, they began charging a dollar a head, man or mule, to go to the river via his Bright Angel Toll Road. But Cameron soon had something his competition did not: a railroad station. Santa Fe pushed a spur line to the Rim in 1901, built hotels in partnership with the Fred Harvey Company and boom! The outlying tourist operations went belly up. Fred Harvey bought up the remaining mule operations by 1904 and, in one corporate form or another, has been running them ever since.

ABOVE AND OPPOSITE: *Mule trains in the early 1900s, photographed by Emery Kolb.*
OPPOSITE, FAR RIGHT: *The Kolb brothers.*

When two young brothers arrived at the Canyon in 1903 intent on setting up a photographic business, Cameron was kind enough to grant them a spot on one of his mining claims at the trailhead. The Kolb brothers, Emery and Ellsworth, set up a tent and began photographing the mule riders as they departed each morning. By the time the riders returned, the Kolbs had photographic prints ready to sell them. No easy task—there was no water at the rim and one of the brothers had to run four miles and 2,500 vertical feet down the trail to their darkroom tent at Indian Garden to develop and print the images, then hoof it back to the rim before the mules returned.

The Kolbs soon began building a rambling permanent studio on their tent site. The studio eventually included a large home for Emery and his family, a gift shop, and a theater to show the films of the Kolbs' boat trips through the canyon. The brothers parted company in the mid-1920s, but Emery remained until his death at the age of ninety-six. He continued taking the daily mule photos for over seventy years, and showed his moving pictures for over sixty—the longest-running movie in the history of the world.

Creation and Conservation of Grand Canyon National Park

THEODORE ROOSEVELT, always a lover of nature, became a great conservationist while he was president of the United States. In 1903, Roosevelt visited Grand Canyon, where he urged Americans to "Leave it as it is. You cannot improve on it. The ages have been at work on it, and man can only mar it. What you can do is to keep it for your children, your children's children, and for all who come after you, as one of the great sights which every American if he can travel at all should see." From the canyon he traveled to Yosemite, where he camped with naturalist John Muir. Muir felt a deep spiritual connection with nature and urged Roosevelt to create Yosemite National Park. They also championed the protection of Grand Canyon. Muir was in awe of the canyon's "*colors,* the living, rejoicing *colors,* chanting morning and evening in chorus to heaven!"

Roosevelt proclaimed Grand Canyon a national monument in 1908, without the consent of Congress, to give it more protection. For the next ten years various Grand Canyon National Park bills were fought out between private interests and the government.

John Burroughs, fellow naturalist, conservationist, and friend of Roosevelt and Muir, also understood the need to protect places like Grand Canyon. Burroughs and Muir descended the Bright Angel Trail astride mules in 1909. Burroughs found it "quite worth while to go down into the cañon on mule-back, if only to fall in love with a mule, and to learn what a sure-footed, careful, and docile creature, when he is on his good behavior, a mule can be." Back at the top, Burroughs reflected: "We seemed to have…brought back a deepened sense of the magnitude of the forms, and of the depth of the chasm which we had heretofore gazed upon from a distance."

At long last, Grand Canyon was given the protection it needed. In 1919, President Woodrow Wilson signed the bill creating Grand Canyon National Park. During the Great Depression (1929–1941) a federal program called the Civilian Conservation Corps built trails, picnic shelters, campgrounds, and telephone lines in the canyon.

ABOVE: *Packers climb through the Coconino layer on the Bright Angel Trail.*
BELOW: *Mules are social herd animals and like to play: sometimes they get a little rough.*

OPPOSITE: *John Burroughs and John Muir at the Grand Canyon in 1909.* OPPOSITE INSET: *President Theodore Roosevelt rides a mule at the Grand Canyon.*

OVERLEAF: *Looking down into the Bright Angel Fault from the Bright Angel Trail.*

A few switchbacks below the now-restored Kolb Studio, our muleskinner (one who drives mules), Dave Cuddeback, halts the train to cinch up our saddles and reiterate the rules that Pancho laid down earlier at the corral: keep your mules three to five feet from the mule in front of you, and don't let them eat the bushes along the trail. Perched on the corral rail this morning, Pancho, with his requisite handlebar mustache and thick cowboy drawl, had elaborated:

They start tryin' to eat on ya, pretty soon you'll start gettin' a gap. Pretty soon it's gonna be fifty feet. Five hundred feet. Ten thousand yards. Pretty soon your mule's gonna be way up here, the rest of the mules are gonna be way down there. Keep in mind they're a herd animal. They'll come to their senses sooner or later, figure out they've been left behind. Whaddya think's gonna happen? Huh? Whattya *think's* gonna happen? They're gonna *run!* Ninety miles an hour down the Grand Canyon with you screamin' for your life—'til they get to them other mules down there. And that's not even the worst part. Cause if you're not the guy in the back? There's a whole crowd of people right behind you goin' just as fast as you are. And yer not gonna be too popular.

Pancho is a third-generation Arizona muleskinner. His granddad packed government mules for the Forest Service in the White Mountains. His daddy ran stock for movies and dudes. Pancho came up here six years ago at the behest of his friend, former livery manager Casey Murph, and took over the job when Murph moved on. It's Pancho's job to keep the operation running, give his wranglers their daily assignments, give the spiel at the corral each morning, and pick out the right mule for each dude.

Equines have a deep history at Grand Canyon. At Stanton's Cave, fifty-seven miles up the Colorado River from Phantom Ranch, paleontologists unearthed bones of a small Pleistocene donkey, *Equus Asinus conversidens,* that roamed the Southwest over ten thousand years ago. Although *E.A. conversidens* went the way of mammoths, mastodons, and giant ground sloths, equines returned with the conquistadors in the 1500s. Three hundred years later, prospectors arrived with horses, mules, and burros. The horses soon departed with the disappointed prospectors, the mules became the preferred pack and riding critter on the main cross-canyon trails, and the burros went feral, quickly adapting to the land of their forebears and spreading throughout the canyon.

The most famous burro, of course, was Brighty, an actual turn-of-the-century burro, romanticized in Marguerite Henry's award-winning 1953 *Brighty of the Grand Canyon,* the children's book etched into the memories of most baby boomers and later made into a popular Disney film.

The feral burros reproduced so prolifically that the National Park Service eventually felt compelled to eliminate them for fear that they would outcompete the native bighorn sheep. The simplest way would have been to shoot them, of course, but when word got out the Park was going to "kill Brighty," they sought an acceptable alternative. Fortunately, Cleveland Amory's Fund for Animals came to the rescue in 1979 and sponsored the live removal of over seven hundred burros by cowboy, helicopter, and whitewater raft over the course of two years.

Brighty the Burro

Brighty was a famous feral burro that lived at Grand Canyon from about 1892 to 1922. He was named after Bright Angel Creek, and spent winters in the canyon and summers on the North Rim. Known for enjoying his freedom, Brighty resisted domestication. However, he was very friendly with children, who would spend hours petting and riding him. Brighty also carried water from a spring in the canyon up to the rim for tourists, and helped haul materials to build the Kaibab suspension bridge over the Colorado River. Brighty had the honor of being the first to cross the finished bridge. Brighty even accompanied President Theodore Roosevelt on a mountain lion hunt at the canyon.

The beloved burro was immortalized by Marguerite Henry in her 1953 book *Brighty of the Grand Canyon* and later in the Disney movie of the same name. A life-size bronze statue of Brighty now graces the lobby of Grand Canyon Lodge on the North Rim, bearing an inscription written by Marguerite Henry: "the artist captured the soul of Brighty, forever wild, forever free."

"Hey, folks!" Dave hollers back along our string of mules. "If you'll look up to the left on that big boulder you'll see pictographs, left by the old Pueblo Indians a thousand years ago." Our death grips on the pommels are relaxing just the least bit and our eyes are able to look at something besides the cliff below. On the overhung face of a cream-colored boulder is a small cluster of blood-hued figures—some with bug-like appendages—reminding us of those who came before. These were left, in all probability, by the Ancestral Puebloans, the culture responsible for most of the renowned cliff dwellings in the Four Corners area.

The Puebloans here at the canyon built less grandly but left traces throughout the canyon—pit houses, granaries, rock art— and even pioneered the trail we are riding down. Arriving sometime after A.D. 500, the Puebloans and their South Rim

counterparts, the Cohonina, colonized Grand
Canyon from rim to river until sometime
around A.D. 1150 when environmental change
caused most of them to move on. Modern
Hopi, Zuni, and other Puebloan tribes
continue their bloodline throughout the
Southwest today.

The Puebloans were not the first to settle
at Grand Canyon. Two thousand years earlier,
archaic wanderers tucked figurines made of
split twigs into caves throughout the eastern
canyon. Perhaps these folks were responsible
for the haunting, multi-hued, life-size pictographs in remote
overhangs in the western canyon as well. We may never know for
sure if these ancient ones were ancestral to the Puebloans, or if
they simply hunted, gathered, and wandered into oblivion.

ABOVE AND OPPOSITE: *Bright Angel Fault
and Plateau Point from the top of the Bright
Angel Trail.*

Nor were the Puebloans the last Native Americans in the
canyon. By the 1300s, Paiutes were approaching from the north
and Havasupais and Hualapais were migrating up from the lower
Colorado River. Within another century or two, Navajos were
moving into the eastern rim country from the far north. Although
the Havasupai tribe is the only one still living within the canyon,
Hualapais, Navajos, and Paiutes still inhabit the surrounding rim
country. The bits of rock art we see above the trail are just a
reminder of how sacred the canyon is to these tribes. To them,
and to many modern long-time residents, Grand Canyon is the
holiest place on earth.

"Motivate those mules!" hollers Dave. Unlike his clients, Dave
rides easy in the saddle, one hand loosely holding the reins, the
other around behind him on the mule's rump, his head twisted
around to keep an eye on us. "Git up here, R.S.! Come on mules!"
A great deal of Pancho's talk this morning centered on motivation.
Each rider was issued a small riding crop which, to be politically
correct, we call a mule motivator. Pancho could not overstress

An endangered California condor finds sanctuary at Grand Canyon.

the importance of keeping a tight mule string. A line of running mules with terrified dudes bouncing wildly in their saddles is the ultimate nightmare for a trail guide. That's when people and mules can get hurt. To keep them tight, they occasionally need to know the rider means business. Pancho explained:

Now nobody wants to hurt one of these mules. And that's the last thing I'd ever ask anyone to do—I think more of these mules than I do of most people. I'm the one that sits up all night with 'em when they're sick, I'm the one that makes sure they get fed every day, that they got new shoes on their feet. I take 'em to the dentist every year. I think a lot of these mules and I'd never ask anybody to hurt one. Matter of fact I'd take it pretty personal if anybody ever did. But the thing is, if you think you're gonna hurt one of these thousand-pound mules—every one of 'em weighs at least a thousand pounds,

some of 'em as much as fifteen hundred pounds—you think you're gonna hurt one with a little bitty piece of plastic, you gotta think a lot of yourself. You better get over to Las Vegas and sign yourself up for a cage match, cause yer pretty dang tough. Lemme tell ya these mules are pretty tough. They walk through cactus all day long, they could care less. They try to eat stuff on the trail with thorns an inch and a half long like it was Cheetos. They kick each other for a game. They just grunt and walk off. If I got kicked like that, I'd be in a coma! These guys are tough, I guarantee you ain't gonna hurt one. They're not gonna cross you off their Christmas card list.

So when Dave sees gaps opening in the mule string, he bellows. And we motivate. My steed has a pronounced proclivity for eating the trailside bushes. A yank on the reins, a nudge with my heels, and a whack with my motivator seem to halt the behavior, at least for a minute or two, but I soon come to realize we have a deal. Every time I prevent Wyatt from getting a mouthful of vegetation, he crowds an overhanging cliff and subtly tries to scrape me off his back. He pretends he's not doing it on purpose, but I'm onto him. Trouble is, he's a lot bigger than me and we both know I am pretty much at his mercy. Weighing in at about two-thirds of a ton and a whopping sixteen hands tall, Wyatt is a force of nature. Dave tells me Wyatt's about fifteen years old and has been working this trail for a good ten years. Averaging about one trip to Phantom Ranch a week, not to mention his rim trail rides, that works out to some impressive numbers. This may be Wyatt's five-hundredth trip to the bottom of the canyon. He has hauled me, or someone like me, both down and up a full five hundred vertical miles. And he may have another ten good years in him. In short, I'm not the first dude he's had to train, nor the last, and no amount of cleverness will surprise him.

Wyatt, like the rest of the mules, was born back east and recruited by the Reese Brothers Mule Company of Gallatin,

A quiet and frosty morning at the top of the trail in the Kaibab Limestone.

Tennessee, the country's largest mule brokers. Sales Manager Rufus Reese and his brother Dickie, third-generation proprietors, have been supplying mules to Grand Canyon for decades. They know what to look for and guarantee their steeds. At Grand Canyon, wranglers make sure they are broken and start them out in the pack train. The best graduate to the dude string. "The ones that don't make good dude mules," says Larry Spain, "go to the pack string. That's the bad boys—the pack mules. They don't work out for ridin', that's where they go. They're all tough." Adds Pancho, "We don't ever put any kind of dudes on any mule we don't think's gonna take care of 'em."

AGES OF STONE

Layer by layer we drop deeper into the canyon and into the Earth's history. At the rim we stood on Kaibab Limestone, the quarter-million-year-old cap rock of much of northern Arizona. Laid down in a sea floor in the late Permian Era and composed of zillions of microscopic limey fossil bits, the Kaibab has, in the last several million years, risen to a height of seven thousand feet above sea level. As Wyatt and his fellow mules plod ever downward, we cut into ever older rock layers of sandstone, limestone, and shale. These layers were once beach sands, mud flats, sea floors, and sand dunes. Their names flow into a litany reminiscent of some obscure religion—Kaibab, Toroweap, Coconino, Hermit, Esplanade, Wescogame, Mankatcha, Watahomigi, Redwall, Temple Butte, Muav, Bright Angel, Tapeats—each name representing a distinct, mappable layer of stone older than the one above it. Although most canyon visitors never learn them by name, old-timers here come to know them as old friends. Count on easy walking in the softer layers like the Bright Angel and a stiff climb through the harder ones like the Coconino or the Redwall.

ABOVE: *This mule train is about to go through the second tunnel into the Coconino layer.*
OPPOSITE: *A guide leads her train of dudes down the trail through the Coconino layer.*

"Get ready, folks!" shouts Dave. We're about to plunge off the Redwall Limestone, the sheerest layer in the Canyon and one of the most beautiful. "This is Jacob's Ladder, named for the biblical ladder Jacob wanted to climb toward heaven." We peer dubiously off our mules at the endless switchbacks stacked below us, the tiny trail wandering out across the plateau from the foot of the cliff. "Only thing is," Dave adds, "we're going down the ladder, not up." We chuckle at the implication and ponder the hellish temperatures that summer riders would be descending into about this time. July temperatures at Phantom Ranch have been known to top 120 degrees, and the guides' toughest challenge is dealing

The end of the steep descent down Jacob's Ladder.

Geology of the Grand Canyon

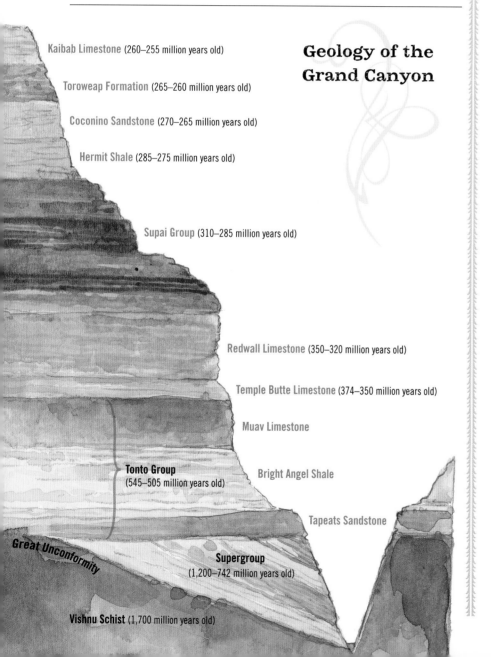

Kaibab Limestone (260–255 million years old)

Toroweap Formation (265–260 million years old)

Coconino Sandstone (270–265 million years old)

Hermit Shale (285–275 million years old)

Supai Group (310–285 million years old)

Redwall Limestone (350–320 million years old)

Temple Butte Limestone (374–350 million years old)

Muav Limestone

Tonto Group
(545–505 million years old)

Bright Angel Shale

Tapeats Sandstone

Great Unconformity

Supergroup
(1,200–742 million years old)

Vishnu Schist (1,700 million years old)

ABOVE AND BELOW: *Switchbacks in the base of the Redwall known as Jacob's Ladder.*

with overheated, dehydrated dudes. Even though we're still shivering, they drill into us the dangers of not drinking enough water. It may be cold, but most of us are out of our element and exerting ourselves in this arid desert climate.

Dave hasn't seen the heat yet—he's a smart one. He works the summers wrangling dudes in the Sierra, where it's cool, and comes to the canyon for the winter months. This coming year, though, he's worked up his nerve to stay here and sweat it out. Wranglers come and go with frequency, the simple reason being they're cowboys and cowgirls at heart. "You know, when you're a cowboy the work's the same pretty much wherever you go," says Larry Spain. "Once you learn the horses and the country, you're ready to go to the next." Nothing makes a cowboy more uncomfortable than getting comfortable.

A Day in the Life of a Grand Canyon Mule

First light and out of the Yaki Barn. The beginning of the one-day resupply round trip to Phantom Ranch.

In the predawn hours (as early as 3 a.m.) the packers commence their work by opening the barn door to the corral of mules that were placed in the pen the previous afternoon.

Two switchbacks into the day on the South Kaibab Trail. The packers are heading to the bottom of the canyon with the food and gear that were on the manifest for the day. In December a Christmas tree will be added to the load.

Every mule is brushed and readied to saddle while they feed themselves. There are three trips to prepare for every day, with as many as thirty dude's mules to saddle up.

The packers have been gone about an hour when the guides come in at 6 a.m. for the day's assignments and the wrangling of the mules who are scheduled for the dude rides. Which mule goes down the trail or stays in the corral depends upon how many days on the trail they have worked.

One of the guides with the day's string of dude mules heads to the stone corral at the top of the Bright Angel Trail.

In the corral at the Bright Angel trailhead, saddlebags wait to be loaded onto the mules,

Both the pack and dude mules carry two hundred pounds maximum. The mules get rested for all the switchbacks, giving the wrangler an opportunity to interpret the

The view from Plateau Point is hands-down one of the best places at Grand Canyon for its river-to-rim views. The day-ride string hitches here while the dudes eat lunch and walk the kinks out

Naturally curious, this mule has discovered the door to the Phantom Ranch tack and feed room wide open. Packers arrive at Phantom Ranch first, around 8 a.m. Guides and dudes arrive around mid-day. Packers and dudes alike overnight at Phantom Ranch.

The South Kaibab Trail provides fantastic vistas of the Inner Gorge. At Plateau Point and here on Windy Ridge you see it all.

A pack train returns to the South Rim barn on the Bright Angel Trail with Phantom Ranch's trash, backpackers' extra gear, and U.S. mail.

It takes about 45 minutes to shoe a mule. A mule gets shod about every forty-five days or eight times a year, if it doesn't lose a shoe in between. The herd of 150 mules needs roughly 4,800 shoes per year. A mule puts a lot of miles on its shoes, traveling up to eight hundred miles in a year.

After hooves are shod the mane and tail are trimmed to identify the mule as having been seen by the farrier.

This mule will testify that worming medicine tastes bad. The livery manager is holding its head up to help the medication go down.

The salt lick is a means to provide essential nutrients. It is readily available around the corral for those

When all the tack is removed and the mules are released in their corral, they will seek out that one perfect spot to roll around to scratch their backs

At the end of the day, the barn floor needs sweeping before the doors are closed for the night.

ABOVE: *Redbud trees in bloom at Indian Garden.*
LEFT AND OPPOSITE: *Guide and dudes on the Tonto Platform heading toward Plateau Point.*

Switch. Back. Switch. Back. Switch. Back. We drop quickly through the Redwall and the trail levels somewhat as we head out across the Tonto Platform toward the Inner Gorge. Cottonwood trees and scattered cabins appear along the drainage ahead and soon we enter the midway area known as Indian Garden. Here spring water bursts from the ground to form Garden Creek and we stop beneath the cottonwoods for lunch. Before the Anglos arrived here to displace them, Havasupais farmed the area, hence the name. Three thousand feet above us, the rim no longer gives any hint of civilization, and it is hard to believe we started there just hours ago. Grand Canyon, the abstract postcard-like panorama we saw from the rim, has now swallowed us whole and we look up, out, and around with a new appreciation of its magnitude and majesty.

Dave helps each of us down from our mount. It is comical. Although two of our party ride often on their ranch in southern Arizona, the rest of us have not been on a horse or mule in years—if ever. Two-and-a-half hours in the saddle combined with the cold-stiffness of December make for erratic gaits that would be the envy of Monty Python's Ministry of Silly Walks. Once on the ground, most of our stiffness walks out pretty quickly. Lunch is an unimpressive box of snacks that we nevertheless devour, and a short walk to the outhouses is a welcome leg-stretcher. But in a matter of minutes, lest we seize up, we're back in our saddles for the final five miles.

OVERLEAF: *Mule deer among the redbud trees at Indian Garden.*

The afternoon ride begins gently and our confidence grows as we follow Garden Creek through the cottonwood grove and down into ledgy brown narrows of Tapeats Sandstone. This is the bottom layer of the Paleozoic sediments—we have descended through 250 million years of stone into beach sands laid down over a half billion years ago. But we're still nowhere near the bottom. The creek abruptly plunges off a waterfall to our left and we veer to the right across a ridge.

"You thought it was going to be easy riding this afternoon?" shouts Dave with a grin. "Welcome to the Devil's Corkscrew!" A vast gulf opens between Wyatt's ears. In revenge for my relentless interruptions of his grazing, Wyatt chooses this point to show off his edge-walking prowess. Eight hundred feet below trickles Pipe Creek, a tributary to Garden Creek. Imagine riding a tall creature that has chosen to walk the railing atop an eighty-story building.

Mules speak with their ears. Two erect ears indicate an attentive mule, focusing on something of interest: a coyote, a bucket of

TOP: *The Bright Angel Trail twists through a cottonwood grove in the area where the Tapeats Sandstone and Vishnu Schist meet, then further down into the "Furnace," Pipe Creek, and the Colorado River.* ABOVE: *A dude's view of the Devil's Corkscrew switchbacks leading down to the Furnace.*

The Bright Angel Trail drops into the Tapeats Narrows along Garden Creek.

oats, or a new rock in the trail. Ears pressed back against the head tell of a mule's anger, usually at the adjacent mule who is trying to bite him. But the norm is the proverbial flop-eared mule, whose ears bounce casually back and forth, up and down, with his gait. This tells you all is well with the world and the mule is likely daydreaming of his next chance to roll in the dirt at day's end. Wyatt's ears are flopping in rhythm to his shuffle along the edge, showing his utter lack of concern, but not necessarily easing mine. Couldn't he be nonchalant on the inside edge of the trail?

We descend beneath the sandstone into a gnarled black schist, the most ancient of rocks in the Southwest. Unlike the four thousand feet of flat sedimentary rock we have already dropped through, this metamorphosed hodgepodge tells of a massive continental collision 1.7 billion years ago when the entire southwestern portion of our continent was born. For more than one hundred million years, volcanic rock and sediment smashed into the southern margin of North America, building some five hundred miles of new continent. Once the collision eased, another half billion years passed while erosion scraped off the overlying mass, and the tortured, twisted schists, granites, and gneisses rose slowly to the surface. When the sea advanced across this new continent to lay down the Tapeats Sandstone, these rocks were already more than a billion years old. Wyatt could care less—while I'm pondering the antiquity of the earth, he's grabbing another mouthful of prickly branches. I yank him to the left and he plows me into the next overhanging rock. And so we pass the Devil's Corkscrew.

We drop into Pipe Creek and follow it down a mile of tight black canyon that in summer is the dreaded Furnace. We're finally getting warm. Around another bend we come suddenly to the Colorado River—the churning heart of Grand Canyon.

THE RIVER'S EDGE

From its mountainous headwaters in Colorado and Wyoming, the Colorado River carves a 1,450-mile course across the high deserts of the Southwest. But dammed, diverted, and drunk dry by the thirsty states that surround it, only a black, briny trickle escapes Mexico into the Sea of Cortez.

Yet it is this same dry barrenness that allowed Grand Canyon to form. The rainwater that forms most rivers simultaneously erodes and softens the surrounding terrain while nourishing forests and vegetation that bury the landscape. Here it is the opposite: virtually none of the rainwater that creates this river falls here in the desert. So the Colorado's erosive powers cut straight down,

The Colorado River flows through the Inner Granite Gorge at Phantom Ranch.

ABOVE: *A desert bighorn ewe with her twins on the Kaibab Limestone shelf above the Bright Angel Trail tunnel.* RIGHT: *Horn Creek Rapid as seen from Plateau Point.*

walls collapse under their sheer weight, and the sere cliff faces lie exposed to the desert sun for millennia. In human terms the river is eternal and the canyon is ancient beyond words. Geologically, however, the Colorado is a brand new river, settling into this desert course only in the last few million years—Grand Canyon is the jagged notch resulting, due to erode away in a few million more. It is very active geology. During a summer thundershower the walls run red with mud and you can feel the erosion at work.

It was by river that Grand Canyon was first explored and described by one-armed Major John Wesley Powell in 1869. When he and his remaining six men emerged from their thousand-mile, hundred-day exploration, they filled in the last blank spot on the continental map. Powell's journal, published six years later, brought the true magnificence of Grand Canyon to the American consciousness. A decade later Hance, Bass, and others began carting those few that could afford it across the desert from the Santa Fe Railway to the rim, and down into the canyon on their mules.

Until the early 1900s, the delta of Pipe Creek was the end of the Bright Angel Trail. Mules and their riders—men in suits, women in full Victorian dresses—lunched here, gazed upstream at the craggy outline of Zoroaster Temple, posed for photographs, then retreated back up the trail. A variant trail meandered upstream across the Tonto Platform from Indian Garden and dropped to the river near present-day Phantom Ranch. Meanwhile, entrepreneurs from southern Utah improved an old Indian route from the North Rim down Bright Angel Creek to the river, where David Rust established a small camp and strung a tramway across the river for stock and riders. He didn't get much business and his tram was eventually replaced with a tenuous swinging bridge.

In 1919, Grand Canyon became a national park, headquartered at the South Rim Village where the train ended. Ralph Cameron still had a stranglehold on the Bright Angel Toll Road and, as a U.S. Senator, he was tough to dislodge. To circumvent him, the Park built an all-new cross-canyon route. They blasted the South Kaibab Trail along the ridge tops to the river from Yaki Point. On the north side they built the North Kaibab, following much of the old trail, but blasting half-tunnels up through the Redwall to the rim. To connect the two, they replaced the old swinging bridge with the current Kaibab Bridge, hauling all the steel down by mule. The huge cables that suspend the bridge came down coiled on the backs of a series of mules, interspersed with dozens of Havasupais, the latter dashing back and forth to keep the cable running around the switchbacks between the mules.

ABOVE: *Dudes and mules rest on the South Kaibab Trail in the Redwall layer with a view of the Colorado River in the Inner Gorge and the Tonto Platform.* RIGHT: *Packers return home up the South Kaibab Trail after their trip to Phantom Ranch.*

PAGES 36–37: *Hikers enjoy the challenging South Kaibab Trail.*

With his trail now irrelevant, Cameron conceded and the National Park Service rebuilt the Bright Angel as well. The Fred Harvey Company, with good trail access, then developed the primitive Rust's Camp into a rustic but comfortable tourist facility with a cantina, showers, cabins, and at one time, a swimming pool. They named it Phantom Ranch, for Phantom Canyon, a side-gulch just upstream. David Meyers, who has managed Phantom for ten years, runs a small crew year-round. They're as different a breed as muleskinners, often preferring to stay in the canyon on their days off. All their food and supplies come in the same way their trash goes out—by mule. Phantom Ranch may be the last place in the country where letters are postmarked, "mailed by mule."

MAILED BY MULE AT
THE BOTTOM
OF THE
GRAND CANYON
PHANTOM RANCH

LEFT: *Near Phantom Ranch, a Park Service helicopter flies over the Silver Bridge and the Colorado River.* BELOW: *Crossing the Black Bridge into the tunnel on the South Kaibab Trail.*

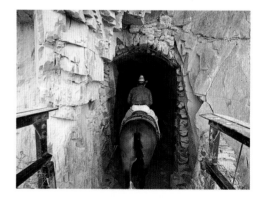

Our mules don't seem to notice the great river but simply turn upstream and plod toward Phantom Ranch along another two miles of sandy trail. "See that silver bridge up ahead?" hollers Dave. Our butts, by now, are getting very tired of our saddles and we eagerly nod, hoping to be across it soon and safely on the ground. "That's not where we're going!" adds Dave. "We've gotta go another mile upriver to the Kaibab Bridge." Our spirits sag. The silver bridge was built in the 1960s to carry a water line that supplies South Rim with water from Roaring Springs, several miles up Bright Angel Creek. A metal mesh above the pipeline allows hikers to cross the bridge, but it is not engineered for mule trains. We can see no conceivable way to get a mule along the

TOP: *The river trail overlooks the Black Bridge and Colorado River.* ABOVE AND RIGHT: *Dudes go through the tunnel entrance to the Black Bridge before crossing it over the river.*

OVERLEAF: *Looking west from Mohave Point into the canyon's entire array of geologic strata.*

sheer cliffs to the upper bridge. But there is a way—in the early 1930s the Civilian Conservation Corps spent two years blasting in the River Trail to connect the foot of the Bright Angel to the Kaibab Bridge. Having reached river level, we figured the cliff-clinging was behind us, but now we find ourselves once again on a narrow, precipitous trail a hundred feet above the river. Even near the bottom of this enormous chasm, you can still be a long way from the ground. On our final descent the trail disappears into a low, dark tunnel. This sometimes gives the mules pause, Dave explains. "But don't get so carried away motivating your

mule that you sit up and smack your head on the low ceiling." Our string tromps on through the tunnel and out onto the bridge without incident. This is child's play compared to crossing the old swinging bridge, or Rust's primitive tram, or worse yet, swimming behind a rowboat.

Now on the north side of the river, we turn up a side canyon and parallel Bright Angel Creek toward Phantom Ranch. In another half mile we'll dismount, clean up, and get ready for a steak dinner at the cantina. Early tomorrow we'll reboard for the long ride out, but it won't be so tough. "It's a lot easier on ya, ridin' uphill," Dave assures us. "You'll walk funny for a while after, but it's not too bad." We want to believe him.

One more difference between mules and horses becomes readily apparent here. A horse, nearing the corral, would begin to trot. A mule could care less. "They'd be content to stay out here on the trail all day," Dave explains. "That's how they are." Our screaming knees and blazing saddle sores make us wish they'd hustle on up to Phantom, but the mules plod on, ears flopping. "These mules have it pretty easy," says Ron Clayton, who managed the operation for decades. "Think of the life of a Kentucky plow mule. They gotta work fourteen hours a day every day—these fellas just go for a hike a couple times a week." Sure, they may do that for twenty years, but hey, that's what mules do. And when they wear out? "Well, they don't really wear out here," Pancho explains. "They get to the point where they're not up for hikin' in and out of Grand Canyon with a heavy load anymore. But they're still good, strong, well-broke mules. We get, I'd say, four phone calls a week lookin' for retired mules. They've got a lot of years left in 'em. They all go to real good homes."

Phantom Ranch

Phantom Ranch, the stopover point for dudes and hikers, sits nearly a mile below the rim. The three corridor trails—the North Kaibab, South Kaibab, and Bright Angel trails—all lead to Phantom Ranch at the bottom of the canyon.

Architect Mary Colter designed this "deepest down ranch in the world" in 1922. She named it after nearby Phantom Creek. The ranch was built of local stone, but all other materials had to be brought in on mules. There were dining and recreation halls, and several small cabins housing up to seventy-five people. Each had two beds, a desk, a fireplace, and an Indian rug on the floor. Colter convinced her fifty-nine-year-old invalid sister Harriet to ride a mule into the canyon for the grand opening.

Today, mules still haul all supplies in and out, including the garbage and U.S. mail. However, Phantom Ranch has grown to include several more buildings, now with electricity and running water.

Guests may experience weather extremes from 120-degree summer days to occasional winter snowfalls. The lower elevation causes Phantom Ranch to stay warmer than Grand Canyon Village, high up on the rim.

ABOVE: *Phantom Ranch guests enjoy some relief from the intense midday heat in cool water under the shade of cottonwood trees.* BELOW: *At first light, the pack train departs Phantom Ranch for the South Rim. Breakfast is eaten in the saddle.*

OPPOSITE, FAR LEFT: *Hikers wait for the doors to open for breakfast at Phantom Ranch's dining hall / store / post office.*

We're so deep in the earth that we see only glimpses of the rim. And we're so deep in time and geologic process that human significance all but vanishes. Certainly Wyatt would agree to that. But as indifferent as my mule seems to me, I've grown quite fond of him and his kin. I can't quite put my finger on it. "Some of 'em have real characters," Larry Spain observes.

They're always gettin' in trouble, they're always messin' around to see what they can get away with. Some of 'em don't wanna be touched, 'I'll do my job, just leave me alone.' Some of 'em are mean. Some of 'em get lazy. Some of 'em never get lazy. Some of 'em got tremendous character, some of 'em are comical, some of 'em like to be petted. We had a mule one time we named Kickapoo—he was good everywhere, except he would kick ya! And he would actually run backwards across that corral to kick at you! You live with 'em, you really get to know 'em.

Mules. "It's nothin' you could explain," says Pancho. "They're their own, you know, deal. They're nothin' like a horse. They just live in their own little world. But if you're lucky enough to get into that world—then you're pretty dang lucky."

Acknowledgments

One October my wife and I were hiking on the South Kaibab Trail when just above the Redwall a mule train of dudes led by a single guide came by. It was neither a surprise nor an unpleasant encounter. We simply thought, "Well, they've passed us, we can continue on now." During that particular sojourn that mule train stuck in my mind as a scene worth getting to know better. Mules are a fixture in Grand Canyon and yet stand apart as a tourist attraction. They are used to access Phantom Ranch by those who would rather ride a mule than walk, or as a beast of burden to carry the heavy loads required to maintain the trails and carry Phantom Ranch's daily supplies in and out, but there seemed to be more and I wanted to find out. Being a photographer by trade, I am always looking for interesting images for my constantly evolving portfolio. I thought the mules and the livery operation based on the South Rim would be a great means of getting to know more about the mules, the guides, and the support crew that makes it all work. After a year of twice-monthly trips to visit the historic mule barns, I have come away with a body of work that hints of the past and is of the present. Along the way friends were consulted and new friends made. It is in that spirit that I would like to acknowledge; Helen Ranney, Kate Brooks, Bill Leibfried, Bob Webb, Ray Brutti, Hazel Clark, Brad Dimock, and my mentor, Jay Dusard.

   This book would not have been possible without the cooperation of the skilled professionals at the South Rim livery operation: Anslem Mann, Bill Carpenter, Buck, Charles Berrong, Colton Candelaria, Dallas McDiffit, David Cuddeback, Gary Williams, Jeremiah Stephan, Joe Marshall, K Bar, Kevin Lenss, Kim Bletsch, Mike Brown, Pancho, Richard Lee, Steve Byrd, and Steve Ordedsen.

—TOM BROWNOLD

About the Photographer & Author

PHOTOGRAPHER TOM BROWNOLD's award-winning photography has been recognized in the 2nd Annual AGFA Photo Gallery, the 2nd Annual American Photo Contest, the 2003 *Geographical Magazine* Photographer of the Year (Landscape Category), the 2004 *Nature's Best Photography Magazine* Photography of the Year (Man in Nature Category), and the International Color Awards Photography Masters Cup in 2007 and 2008. His photography has been featured in numerous books, magazines, and calendars. Tom lives in Flagstaff, Arizona, where he has owned and operated his Tom Brownold Photography business since 1995.

WRITER BRAD DIMOCK has worked as a river guide in Grand Canyon and rivers throughout the world for more than 35 years. He is a noted authority on the history of Grand Canyon and the Colorado River and has written articles and essays for national magazines, edited and coauthored several books, and written three National Outdoor Book Award books, including *Sunk Without a Sound: the Tragic Colorado River Honeymoon of Glen and Bessie Hyde.* He lives in Flagstaff, Arizona, where he writes, runs rivers, and builds boats.

Resources

SOUTH RIM MULE RIDES

Xanterra South Rim, L.L.C.
P.O. Box 699, Grand Canyon, Arizona 86023
(928) 638-2631
www.grandcanyonlodges.com

NORTH RIM MULE RIDES

Canyon Trail Rides
P.O. Box 128, Tropic, Utah 84776
(435) 679-8665
www.canyonrides.com

GENERAL INFORMATION

Grand Canyon National Park
P.O. Box 129, Grand Canyon, AZ, 86023
(928) 638-7888
www.nps.gov/grca